P9-DGV-800

Gifts
from the
Enemy

by Trudy Ludwig
Illustrated by Craig Orback

Based on *From a Name to a Number: A Holocaust Survivor's Autobiography*
by Alter Wiener

WHITE CLOUD PRESS / The HumanKIND™ Project
Ashland, Oregon

Copyright text © 2014 by Trudy Ludwig.
Copyright illustrations © 2014 by Craig Orback.
All rights reserved. No part of this book may be used or reproduced in any manner whatsoever without written permission except in the case of brief quotations embodied in critical articles and reviews.

Gifts from the Enemy is a nonfiction picture book based on *From a Name to a Number: A Holocaust Survivor's Autobiography* by Alter Wiener.

White Cloud Press titles may be purchased for educational, business, or sales promotional use. For information, please write:

White Cloud Press / The HumanKIND™ Project
PO Box 3400
Ashland, OR 97520
www.whitecloudpress.com

Illustrations by Craig Orback. The illustrations in this book were rendered in oil paint.
Cover and interior design by Craig Orback and C Book Services

Printed in South Korea

14 15 16 17 18   10 9 8 7 6 5 4 3 2 1

Library of Congress Cataloging-in-Publication Data

Ludwig, Trudy, author.

Gifts from the enemy / by Trudy Ludwig.

    pages cm

"Based on From a Name to a Number: A Holocaust Survivor's Autobiography by Alter Wiener"--Publisher.

Includes bibliographical references and index.

ISBN 978-1-935952-97-8 (hardcover : alk. paper)

1. Wiener, Alter, 1926- 2. Jews--Poland--Chrzanów--Biography--Juvenile literature. 3. Holocaust, Jewish (1939-1945)--Personal narratives--Juvenile literature. 4. Holocaust survivors--Oregon--Portland--Biography--Juvenile literature. I. Orback, Craig, illustrator. II. Title.

DS134.42L83 2014

940.53'18092--dc23

    [B]

                                    2014007532

There are those who say that what I've lived through never happened. But I'm here to tell you that it did. My name is Alter Wiener and I am an ordinary person with an extraordinary past.

Many years ago, I was young like you. I lived with my family in Chrzanów, a small town in the southwest corner of Poland.

Back then, our home had no indoor plumbing. We had no refrigerators, cell phones, TVs, or computers. We didn't even own a car. We mostly walked to get where we needed to go.

It was a much simpler way of life. Still, our home was full of books, food, laughter, and love.

Every Friday Papa invited a poor student or a homeless person to share our Sabbath dinner with us. At sunset, we welcomed the Sabbath with the blessing and lighting of candles, followed by the blessing of Mama's freshly baked challah. I couldn't wait to get a slice of the bread, all soft and warm in my hands. Biting into it was pure heaven!

Mama was a wonderful cook. She spent hours in the kitchen, preparing mouth-watering meals for Papa, my brothers Shmuel, Hirsh, and me.

Mama also had a caring heart. "There are two ways to deal with the cold," she'd often say. "Put on a fur coat to be warm, or light a fire so that others can be warm, too."

Mama made sure we provided food and shelter to those less fortunate than us—both in times of peace and, later, during the war.

On September 1, 1939, German Nazi soldiers, under orders of their leader, Adolf Hitler, attacked my country. Poland's army wasn't strong enough to defend our borders and people. Thousands of us tried to flee, including my own family, but we had nowhere to go. Hitler's army had us surrounded.

Papa, a thoughtful, peaceful man, taught my brothers and me to reject hatred. Hitler taught his people to embrace it.

Their hatred started with words—hurtful words first whispered, then shouted at neighbors and strangers alike. Those words took root in the hearts and minds of many and grew into something worse.

When Hitler came into power, he ordered his army to seek out, imprison, and destroy millions of people, old and young, who looked, thought, and acted differently than his people. Hitler hated differences.

The German army's occupation was hard on everyone in our town, but it was the hardest on the Jewish people because we were on the top of Hitler's hate list.

Our freedom and rights were taken away.

We couldn't go to school.

We couldn't pray in our houses of worship.

We couldn't even visit our favorite parks or playgrounds.

Curfews forced us to be prisoners in our own homes.

Many good and decent people lost their lives to this hatred—including my own friends and family.

I was 13 years old when the German soldiers marched into town and killed poor Papa.

I was 14 when, in the middle of the night, they forced their way into our home and took my older brother Shmuel away.

I was 15 when the Nazis came for me. I didn't even have the chance to hug Mama and little Hirsh good-bye. It was the last time I would ever see them again.

I and many others were herded like cattle onto trains headed to destinations far, far away from kindness, compassion, respect, and dignity.

I was shipped from one prison labor camp to another, living in very crowded, dirty conditions. Day after day, I was forced to work long hours. The guards showed no mercy in their cruel treatment of the prisoners. And there was never enough food to eat. I was always hungry. So very hungry. I kept thinking about Mama and her wonderful challah. I would have done anything to have just one small taste of home-baked bread.

Months went by. Then years. Lack of food and so much suffering kept my belly empty and my heart heavy.

Just when I no longer had the strength or will to make it through another day, something amazing happened: I received gifts from a stranger. Not just any stranger. A stranger who I thought was my enemy.

It happened when I was working in a German factory. Posted on the factory's walls were signs addressed to all German employees:

> **Do not look at the prisoners.**
> **Do not talk to the prisoners.**
> **Do not give anything to the prisoners.**
> **If you do, you will be DOOMED.**

One day, a German worker made eye contact with me. When she saw she had my attention, she pointed her finger at a box on the floor. Curious, I went to that spot when no one was looking and peeked under the box.

What did I find? The most wonderful gift I could ask for … a bread and cheese sandwich! I couldn't believe my eyes! I grabbed the sandwich and gobbled it up before anyone noticed.

Even more surprising, this worker left me a bread and cheese sandwich under that very same box every day for the 30 days that I worked in her building!

Why, I asked myself, would this stranger be willing to risk her life not once but 30 times for me? Why me? Did she have a son my age and feel sorry for me? Was she a religious person who believed it was her duty to help the helpless?

To this day, I don't know her reason for feeding me. What I do know is that she gave me the energy and hope to survive. Her acts of kindness also made me stop and think: How can I believe all Germans are my enemy when this woman, a German, had risked her life for me? That's when I learned my most important lesson in life: There are the kind and the cruel in every group of people. How those you meet in life treat you is far more important than who they are.

In May 1945, the Russian army arrived at our camp, telling us that the war was over, Germany was defeated, and we were free at last! I tried to track down the identity of my brave German hero, but I couldn't find her. Still, not a day goes by when I don't think of this wonderful woman and thank her for her courage and kindness.

It has been many years since the war. I am much older now, but my memories of the past are still strong. Every Friday at sunset, I welcome the Sabbath with the lighting and blessing of candles, followed by the blessing of challah. Now, when I bite into the bread, I don't just taste heaven. I taste freedom.

Afterword

There is an old saying that a smart person learns from his or her own experiences, but a wise person also learns from the experiences of others. Many people who have heard my presentations in churches, synagogues, schools, and correction facilities, as well as readers of my autobiography, *From a Name to a Number*, have personally shared with me the positive impact my life story has had on their lives. "Your story must be retold to the old *and* the young," they say. "Present and future generations must remember the Holocaust, learn from it, and do everything possible to prevent another genocide from happening again."

Hatred Has No Borders

In the Second World War, every Jew was a victim, but not every victim was a Jew. Priests, clerics, Jehovah's Witnesses, Roma, Afro-Germans, Russians, Czechs, Poles, Serbs, political dissidents, people with disabilities, and many others were also on Hitler's hate list. Because Hitler believed Germans were members of a superior human race of people he called "Aryan," he regarded all non-Aryans *untermentchen* (subhuman), to be subjugated and some, particularly the Jews, to be destroyed. Many Germans, fearful of being punished for disagreeing with their *führer* (leader), succumbed to his racist ideology.

The readers of *Gifts from the Enemy* are children who have probably never experienced what I had been subject to as a youth. In Waldenburg concentration camp, for example, the Nazis took away my name and gave me a number. Instead of warm clothes, socks, and boots to protect me from inclement weather, I was supplied with only a threadbare uniform and wooden clogs. My bunk bed—a narrow plank of wood with no mattress, pillow, or sheets—also served as my table and chair. There were no dishes, cups, or glasses. My only utensil was a shallow metal bowl for what little food was given to me. I had no towel, comb, or toothbrush. I could not see my face because I had no mirror. Instead, all my eyes could see was human suffering.

Throughout my teenage years, I did not live; I could hardly exist. The only right I had was the right to die. For over five years, I was subjected daily to atrocities—not for what I did but for who I was.

It is my hope that *Gifts from the Enemy* will help young readers to understand that both the wicked and the virtuous can be found in every group of people. Stereotyping or sweeping guilt by association is unfair and unjust. Who knows how further along our civilization would be if all those lives lost had, instead, been allowed to flourish. It is also my strong wish for today's children to never give up hope in their efforts to make this world a better, more caring place for all.

—Alter Wiener, author of *From a Name to a Number: A Holocaust Survivor's Autobiography*

The Holocaust & A World at War

The Holocaust is a term used to describe the persecution and mass killings of approximately six million European Jews during World War II. When Adolph Hitler, the leader of the Nazi Party, rose to power in Germany in the early 1930s, he and his supporters blamed primarily the Jewish people for their country's problems and regarded them as an "inferior race." By convincing his followers that the Jews and many other groups of people were a threat to the German nation and race, Hitler paved the way for atrocities to be committed against millions of innocent men, women, and children.

In this war, which lasted from 1939 to 1945, the European Jews weren't the only ones who suffered. Hitler and his allies' attempt at global domination involved many nations, resulting in the loss of over 50 million lives worldwide. With the fighting spread throughout Europe, Northern Africa, Asia, the Atlantic and Pacific Oceans, as well as the Mediterranean Sea, World War II is considered to be the most widespread, destructive war in the history of mankind.

Vocabulary

Sabbath: The day of rest and religious observance for Jews and some Christians, which starts every Friday at sunset and ends on Saturday at sunset.

Challah: Yeast-leavened egg bread that's often braided prior to baking and traditionally eaten by Jews on the Sabbath and holidays.

Nazis: Members of Germany's national political party led and controlled by Adolph Hitler from 1933 to 1945. Under Hitler's Nazi dictatorship, the citizens in his country were denied basic rights including freedom of speech, religion, and political beliefs. At the end of WW II, the Nazi political party was outlawed in Germany.

Occupation: The control of a country by the physical presence of a foreign military power.

Houses of worship: Places where people of a particular religious faith gather to pray.

Curfew: A law or rule that requires people to stay off the streets and remain indoors at certain times of the day and/or night.

Prison labor camp: A place where prisoners are forced to live and perform physical work inside and outside the camp.

Genocide: The deliberate, systematic killing of a national, ethnic, racial, or religious group of people.

Questions for Discussion

…I am an ordinary person with an extraordinary past.

- Before the German army invaded Poland, in what ways was Alter's family life similar to yours? How was his family life different from yours?

- Do you think Alter's parents were kind and caring people? Give some examples from the story to support your answer.

- How did the German army occupation of Alter's home town affect the daily lives of the Jewish townspeople?

- What was Alter's life like when he was a prisoner?

Their hatred started with words—hurtful words first whispered, then shouted at neighbors and strangers alike. Those words took root in the hearts and minds of many and grew into something worse.

- Have you ever been treated poorly or called names because of how you look, dress, think, or act? If yes, how did that make you feel?

- When you see others being treated poorly, what do you think they're feeling?

- Do you believe that hurtful words and name-calling have the power to build up or break down the human spirit? If yes, explain.

- How can hurtful words lead to hurtful actions?

There are the kind and the cruel in every group of people. How those you meet in life treat you is far more important than who they are.

- What happened in Alter's life that got him to still have faith in the goodness of people, despite having experienced such horrors in the prison camps?

- Why do you think the German stranger risked her life to feed Alter when she was ordered not to?

- Many people may not feel safe taking big risks to help out others, as Alter's kind German stranger had done, but we are all capable of performing some small act of kindness without risking our own safety. What act of kindness have you done recently or can you now do to make a positive difference in someone else's life?

Recommended Activities for Young Readers

Appreciating Similarities & Differences

Divide the students into groups for this compare and contrast exercise. Give the students 90 seconds to write down on paper a list of what they have in common with the peers in their particular group (e.g., they each have a brother in their family, they all play a musical instrument, they all love soccer, they are all wearing pants, etc.).

   When the 90 seconds are up, have them turn the paper over. On the reverse side, have each group take 90 seconds to write a list of what they don't have in common with one another in their group (e.g., only one child in the group wears glasses, has curly hair, has a pet rabbit, speaks Japanese, etc.).

   Have the groups compare their similarities list length with their differences list length. Have them discuss which list was easier and quicker to write.

Lesson learned / shared: We all have something in common with others. We need to focus on our similarities and learn to appreciate and respect our differences.

> *"Our greatest strength as a human race is our ability to acknowledge our differences, our greatest weakness is our failure to embrace them."*
> Judith Henderson

Promoting Acts of Kindness:

- **Create Kindness Journals**
  Provide children with supplies to create and decorate their own kindness journals. Encourage them to perform acts of kindness on a daily basis for one or two weeks. Have them record in their journals:
  > … acts of kindness they have done for others they may or may not know and how performing those acts made them feel;
  > … acts of kindness they have received from others and how those acts of kindness made them feel.

- **Support Worthwhile Causes / Organizations**
  Encourage a small or large group of children to come together to help support a larger population in need. For example, they could draw pictures or write letters and poems to comfort the elderly or patients in children's hospitals, contribute supplies to local food banks and homeless shelters, or raise funds for a disaster relief organization.

Lesson learned / shared: Our acts of kindness—whether performed individually or as a collective group—have the power to make a positive impact on the lives of others.

> *"Once you begin to acknowledge random acts of kindness—both the ones you have received and the ones you have given—you can no longer believe that what you do does not matter."*
> Dawna Markova

Dedication

Thank you, Alter Wiener, for encouraging youth and adults to do better, to be better, in how they treat their fellow human beings—regardless of race/ethnicity, sexual orientation, and political or religious beliefs.

Our heartfelt gratitude to Sprigeo; the Anti-Defamation League; Calvary Christian School; Kelly Hock; Annette McQueen; Laura Barbour; the Butcher-DeLoughery family; the Long family; the Ludwig clan; Alison Lovell and family; Dan Larson and family; Robert, Heidi and Josh Klonoff; Emily and Olivia Fouser; Michele Borba; Larry Magid; Anne Collier; Robert, Joan, Erik, Anja and Luke Larson; Gary and Eileen Orback; Jill Slansky; Nancy Willard; Belinda Zeidler; Leslee Dillon and Chris Viehoff; Gretchen Olson; Greg Carter and Randy Wampler; and all our wonderful Kickstarter supporters, friends, colleagues, educators, counseling professionals, and caring adults and kids out there who believe in the power of our words and actions to plant the seeds of change in the world.

Last but not least, this book is also dedicated to Alter Wiener's brave German hero, who risked her life to nourish his. May we all never underestimate how acts of kindness—no matter how big or small—can make a positive difference in the lives of those we touch.

–T.J.L.

For my grandmother Ethel Schneider (May 13, 1915–December 19, 2012), who also lived through monumental times.

–C.S.O.